This is

SKUnK

They love to play the drums.

Say their names together,

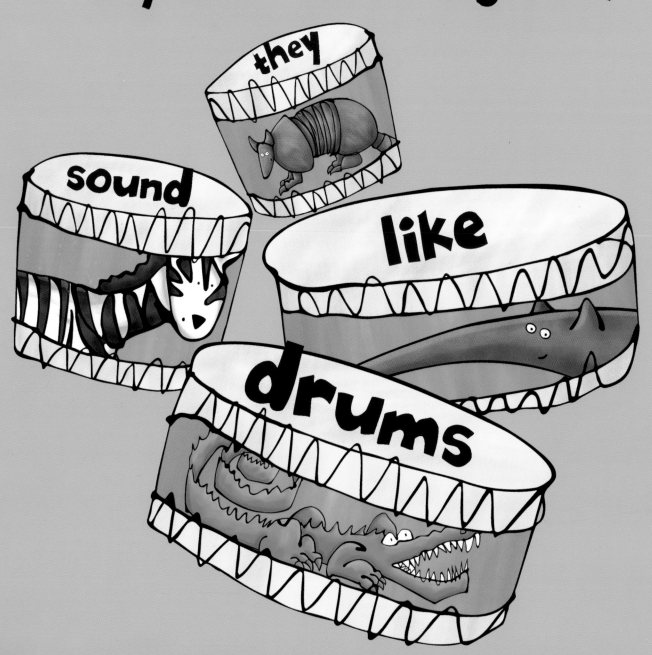

they sound like drums

Steve Webb

Tanka Tanka Skunk!

Sounds like drums

This is
Tanka

like this...

Skunka Tanka

Skunka Tanka

Tanka Tanka Skunk!

They've got the beat, and so have their friends.

This is kangaroo.
His name has three
beats, like this…

And this is caterpillar.
His name has four
beats, like this...

cat- er- pil- lar

They've lots more friends for you to meet.
Say their names, to the Skunka Tanka beat.

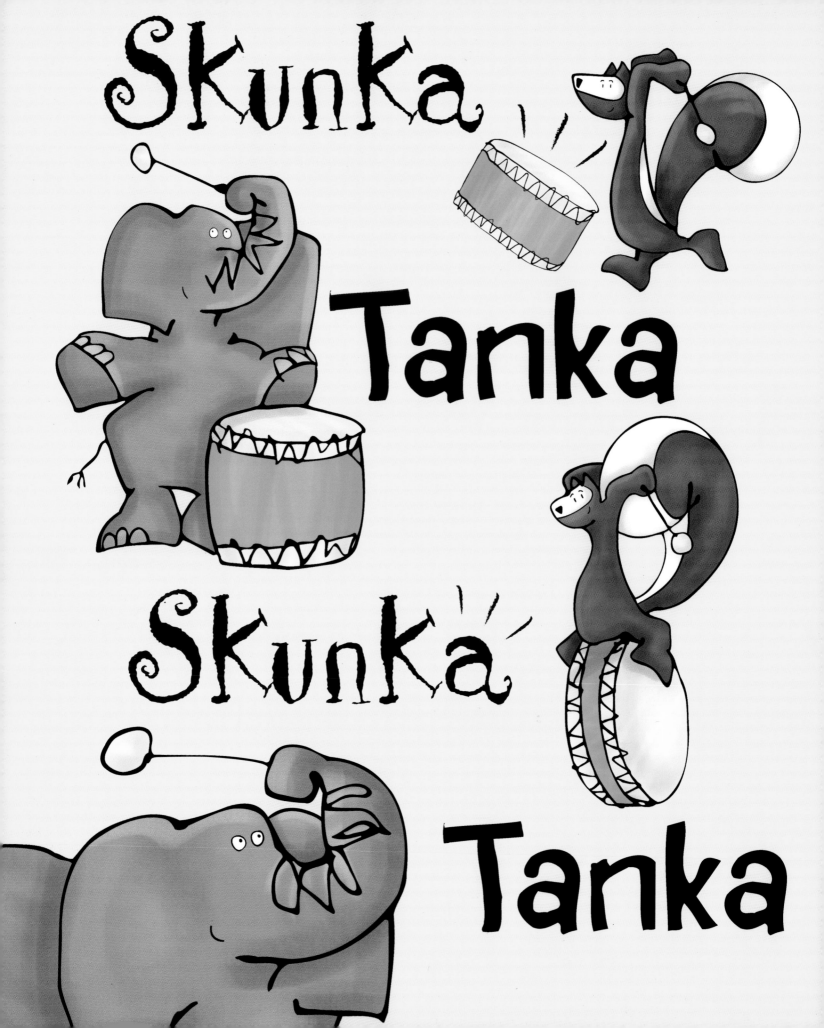

Tanka

Tanka

Tanka

SKunK!

tiger

cheetah

tiger

cheetah

panda

polar bear

lemur

llama

llama

lemur

zebra

badger

BAT

cat- er- pil- lar

BIG
GORILLA

YAKETY

YAKETY

YAK

beaver

otter

badger

beaver

dingo

donkey

DUCK

panda

panther

tiger

zebra

alligator

FOX

tiny little hairy spider

armadillo

OX

Skunka

Tanka

Skunka

Tanka

ant-

eater

BIG BLUE

ant-

eater

WHALE

Skunka
Tanka
Skunka
Tanka

Once more from the top...

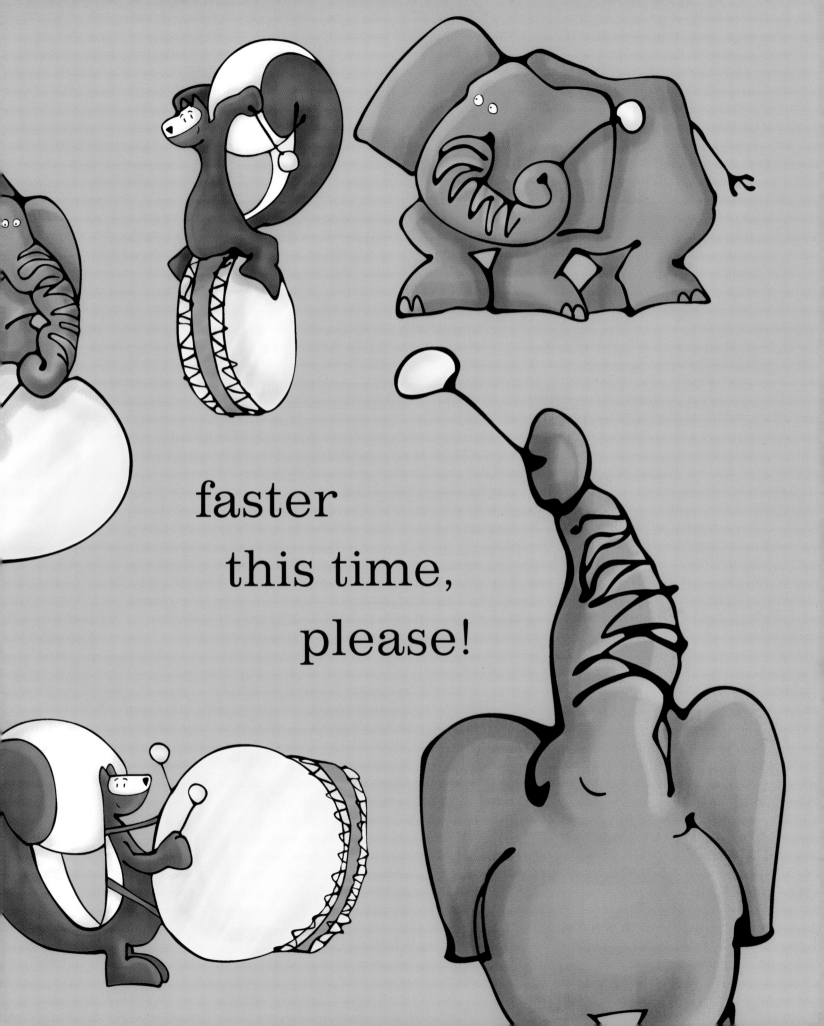

faster
this time,
please!

For my very favourite people
in all the world,
Sam, Hannah and Kate.
Hats off to Ernie,
and 'bonsoir' to Badger...

TANKA TANKA SKUNK!
A RED FOX BOOK 978 0 09 943977 6

First published in Great Britain by Hutchinson,
an imprint of Random House Children's Books

Hutchinson edition published 2003
Red Fox edition published 2004

5 7 9 10 8 6 4

Copyright © Steve Webb, 2003

Red Fox Books are published by Random House Children's Books,
61–63 Uxbridge Road, London W5 5SA,
A RANDOM HOUSE GROUP COMPANY
Addresses for companies within The Random House Group Limited can
be found at:www.randomhouse.co.uk/offices.htm

THE RANDOM HOUSE GROUP Limited Reg. No. 954009
www.**kids**at**r**andomhouse.co.uk
www.tankatankaskunk.co.uk

A CIP catalogue record for this book is available from the British Library.

Printed in China